ASK PIPPA

Pippa Funnell began riding when she was very young – on a pony lent to her by a friend of her mother's.

An Olympic champion, she became the first and (so far) only person to win eventing's greatest prize, the Rolex Grand Slam in 2003, riding Primmore's Pride.

She has had countless other successes in her career, most recently winning the Bramham International Horse Trials on Redesigned in June 2010. She's also delighted to have been a member of the British team at the 2010 World Equestrian Games held in Kentucky.

Pippa is proud to be a trustee of World Horse Welfare. Visit their website at www.worldhorsewelfare.org.

Pippa lives in Surrey with her husband, William Funnell, a top class show jumper.

0000004

D1614572

Have you discovered the Tilly's Pony Tales books by Pippa Funnell?

Tilly Redbrow doesn't just love horses, she lives, breathes and dreams them too! Warm, engaging stories packed with Pippa's expert advice on everything you ever wanted to know about horses.

Magic Spirit the Dream Horse
Red Admiral the Racehorse
Rosie the Perfect Pony
Samson the Stallion
Lucky Chance the New Foal
Solo the Super Star
Pride and Joy the Event Horse
Neptune the Heroic Horse
Parkview Pickle the Naughty Show Pony
Nimrod the Circus Pony
Moonshadow the Derby Winner
Autumn Glory the New Horse
Goliath the Rescue Horse
Buttons the Naughty Pony
Rusty the Trustworthy Pony *(September 2011)*
Royal Flame the Police Horse *(November 2011)*
Stripy the Zebra Foal *(January 2012)*
Free Spirit the Mustang *(March 2012)*

Visit the Tilly's Pony Tails website at
www.tillysponytails.co.uk

ASK PIPPA

Pippa Funnell

Orion
Children's Books

First published in Great Britain in 2011
by Orion Children's Books
a division of the Orion Publishing Group Ltd
Orion House
5 Upper St Martin's Lane
London WC2H 9EA
An Hachette UK Company

1 3 5 7 9 8 6 4 2

A catalogue record for this book is available from the British Library.

ISBN 978 1 4440 0265 2

Printed in Great Britain by
Clays Ltd, St Ives plc

www.orionbooks.co.uk
www.tillysponytails.co.uk

*To all the wonderful horses
I have been fortunate enough to
have worked with over the years*

Dear Reader,

Before you start reading this book, I want to personally thank you all for sending in questions. I also just want to explain that many of these answers come from my own experiences with horses. People have different views, they do things differently, and we all have different systems that work for us, so the answers here are from my view point and what I have found works for me and my horses.

I have always tried to stay open-minded, trying out new ideas, seeing if they work or not. One thing is for sure, you never stop learning with horses.

Of course, many of us will have limitations and some may not have the same facilities as others, but I believe that good overall horse management is not about which horse has the smartest rug or biggest stable, it's about giving them the love and care they need.

Finally, one thing we must all remember is that however stressful things get, we choose to be involved with horses and ponies for our own enjoyment. We must never forget that, no matter how much we might want to do something, we have to ask whether it is in our horse's best interests, and we must always remember that horses are not machines. They are individuals in their own way and we must respect that in order for us all to stay happy, confident and above all SAFE.

Happy reading, and happy riding!

ABOUT
HORSES

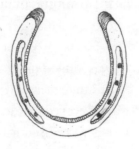

Can you tell us a bit about the history of horses?

It was over five thousand years ago when people decided that they might be able to train and ride horses. Wild horses originally roamed free in herds, but there was always a pecking order. A stallion would keep watch and protect his herd. These wild horses were eventually captured and tamed by humans for domestic use. Fast, 'warm-blooded' horses were a means of travel, and from the beginning changed the way men hunted. They carried soldiers to war, pulled chariots in Egypt, and later, drew beautiful carriages for the nobility and became a form of everyday transport. Slower, 'cold-blooded' horses were used for labour, helping farmers with their planting and other work. There are approximately seventy-five million horses in the world today, and many different breeds. Now, while there are still numerous working horses, the gracefulness, agility, speed and strength of horses mean that they are also used for both pleasure and competitions.

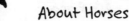 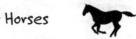

Do horses like being ridden?

Yes, I think horses do enjoy their work. It is important to keep the work varied in order to keep their enjoyment and interest levels up. We turn our horses out in the field as well, so that they can have some essential natural horse time. If you keep your horse's work interesting, fun and within his capabilities then he should stay confident and happy.

Why are horses measured in "hands", and what does it mean?

A hand is a unit of measurement of length equal to 4 inches or 10.16 centimetres. It was originally based on the breadth of a male hand in the days before we had tape measures. A horse is measured from its feet in a straight line up to the highest point of the withers. Try to stand your horse up square on firm, level ground. Once you have his height in inches, you divide by four to get his measurement in hands.

3

What's the difference between a horse and a pony?

A pony is a small horse that measures less than 14.2 hands high (hh) at the withers. Ponies can be as small as 38 inches (9.2hh) – but the smallest pony ever recorded was a tiny 17 inches (4.1hh). Horses can go up to about 18hh. The largest horse ever recorded was a shire called Mammoth, who was 21.2hh.

Most children learn to ride on ponies and then progress on to horses. Compared to horses, ponies often have thicker manes, tails and coats overall, as well as proportionally shorter legs, wider barrels, heavier bone, thicker necks, and shorter heads with broader foreheads.

What is the average life expectancy for a horse?

Approximately twenty to thirty years, though ponies tend to live longer than horses.

How can you tell a horse's age?

You can estimate a horse's age by his teeth. When horses are born they have a couple of milk teeth, and by the time they are two years old they have a full set. These milk teeth are gradually replaced by permanent teeth, usually by the age of five. After the age of five, the age of a horse can be guessed by studying the shape of the teeth, the angle at which they meet, and general wear and tear, but it is not an exact science, and as they get older it becomes more difficult to age them.

How can you tell what a horse is thinking?

The easiest way to tell what a horse is thinking is by looking at his ears. When his ears are pricked forwards he is alert, happy and interested. When the ears are flat back against his neck, it usually means he is unhappy or annoyed. When his ears are slightly lowered to the side it means he is relaxed, and if his ears are flickering it means he is listening and attentive.

I also think when you know your horse well, you can read his body language and his expression. You'll be able to see in his eyes whether he looks happy and relaxed, or anxious and worried, or even mischievous.

What does it mean when a horse has "good conformation"?

A horse with good conformation makes our job easier! Like people, no horse is perfect, but a well put together horse is more likely to be athletic, well balanced and hopefully stay sound. His neck, back and hip should all be the same length, and there should be a straight line from the top of the front of his legs all the way down to the middle of his hooves. It's good to imagine your horse fitting into a square box. He should have the right amount of bone in proportion with his body. In other words, you don't want a big-framed horse on spindly legs, but with a fine thoroughbred you don't mind.

I have evented many horses with slight conformational faults, but the most important thing is that they can be trained and have a big heart. It's obviously more important for a show horse to have good conformation because that makes up a lot of the marks when being judged.

I know that horses are herd creatures, but do they mind being on their own?

Horses generally prefer to have other horses around them, but it very much depends on the individual horse as to whether they need company.

Some of our horses hate being left on their own in the lorry, whereas others don't mind at all. Our ridden horses are all put out to grass individually, but will normally have other horses in fields next to them. All our homebreds are brought up in herds until they are broken in and get hind shoes on, and then they go on their own in case they get kicked.

In winter when my horses have a proper holiday, they all go out together.

My horse sometimes bites or kicks the other horses in the field. Should I be worried?

It is pretty natural for one horse to be the boss –
that's how they decide a pecking order – and the
others do normally learn to keep their distance. If
you think he is being too aggressive it might be
better to regroup the horses, because he could
be trying to protect a mare or a particular friend.
If he behaves like this mainly when you are
around, maybe at feed time or if you have titbits,
then you could consider removing him from the
field at feed times so he doesn't have to bite or
kick to get his share, or upset the other horses
and stop them from getting their fair share.

How can I tell if my horse is healthy? What should I look for?

A healthy horse should be bright and interested in his surroundings. His coat should be sleek and shiny and his eyes bright and fully open. His nostrils should be dry and clean. He should have a healthy appetite and drink between five and ten gallons of water a day. When you pinch the skin on your horse's neck, if it takes longer than about a second to go back, this could indicate dehydration. All horses are different so try to get to know your own horse as much as possible – that way it will be easier to pick up if he is unwell.

My mum's horse has got laminitis. How can we prevent it from coming back?

Laminitis is a painful foot condition, when the membranes that hold the bone of the foot in place (the laminae) become inflamed, and it is one of the most common causes of lameness and disability in horses and ponies.

There are lots of reasons why a horse might get laminitis, and obviously prevention is better than cure. Be careful about his diet. Avoid rapidly growing or fertilised grass, and maybe limit your horse's grass intake by using a grazing muzzle. Try not to let him get overweight. You should be able to feel his ribs and he should not have a hard crest. Finally, ensure that rich, concentrated food is locked away so there's no risk of your horse gorging on it.

What is mud fever and what would you recommend to cure it?

Mud fever is a difficult and painful disease affecting a horse's lower legs. It is a common condition that affects horses in the winter, when they are living or working in wet, muddy conditions. The skin over the pasterns and heels becomes infected and then scabby and painful. White limbs are particularly susceptible because they don't have colour pigment to protect the skin. Once again, prevention is better than cure, so try and keep your horse's legs dry and grease his heels with a barrier cream to keep the moisture out. If you wash your horse's legs, always dry them properly afterwards. We get some "magic" pink lotion from our vet, which contains cortisone and antibiotics, and put this on our horses' legs and then bandage over the top, but this can only be used out of the competition season.

About Horses

Why doesn't being shod hurt a horse or pony when it's done with fire and nails?

Hot shoeing doesn't hurt a horse at all. Our young horses get held when they are first shod because they can get scared by the smoke. If you were to grow out your finger nail, you could put a nail through it without any pain; but if you pushed the nail through the soft tissue of your finger, it would hurt. When horse shoes are nailed in, they are nailed at an angle so the horse doesn't feel it. Bad shoeing can ruin a good horse so make sure you have a good farrier.

What does it mean when a horse "crib-bites"?

Crib-biting is when a horse uses his teeth to grab onto the top of the stable door or manger. Then if he arches his neck and swallows air this is called wind-sucking.

Crib-biting can cause abnormal wear on your horse's teeth and some people think it's caused by boredom and not getting enough exercise.

What do horses eat and how often should I feed my horse?

Horses are grazing animals and tend to eat little and often. If your horse lives out (i.e. not in a stable), it depends how much grass you have as to how much extra roughage or hard feed to give him. You need to feed according to size, type, age, condition and the sort of work he does. (See page 40.)

Our stabled horses get a full net of haylage (a hay replacement made from semi-dried grass) twice a day and then they are fed twice a day too. Many people feed more, but for practical reasons, because of the number of horses we have, we just give them two feeds, unless one needs more.

They need a balanced diet, which you get in most branded nuts and mixes. And of course all horses enjoy extra treats like apples, carrots and polos!

Ask Pippa

Is it okay to give my pony treats?

We don't give our horses treats all the time because it can make them nip.

But I do have a habit, particularly after I've been away, of going round to all of mine giving them polos. It makes me feel as though they're pleased to see me.

When competing, we give our horses a treat after dressage or showjumping, but it's best not to do it straight after cross-country or heavy work when they're still puffing, in case it causes them to choke.

Do horses need more food if they are doing more exercise?

You can't expect a car to work without petrol, and it's the same for horses.

If our horses are having a quiet time, we would cut down their feed and gradually increase it as we increase their work.

It will depend on whether the horse is slightly excitable or lazy as to how much carbohydrate and protein they are given. We feed all our horses according to their individual needs.

I do monitor them closely and give them more or less hay depending on how they look.

Ask Pippa

What is concentrated feed and should I be giving this to my horse?

Concentrated feed is also known as hard feed. Concentrates include oats, barley, maize, linseed, chaff, bran and sugarbeet.

You might need to give your horse hard feed in the summer, when he will probably be doing more strenuous work, as well as during the winter, when there's very little grass for grazing and it gets really cold.

There are lots of good pre-mixed feeds on the market these days that will suit a variety of horses and ponies, so you don't have to buy different straight feeds any more.

You can always get advice from the nutritionalists who work for feed companies, and they will be able to tell you what they think your individual horse needs.

How can I protect my pony from those pesky flies?

Flies can be very annoying in the summer. In the wild, horses generally have long manes, tails and forelocks which help flick flies away.

In the field, you could use fly rugs and masks made of mesh, which prevent the flies from getting in, but means the horses can still look out.

When competing, we use a good fly spray, which we spray on their bodies and then use a cloth to apply it around their ears and eyes.

What is colic and how should I treat it? What should I look out for?

Colic is, essentially, a stomach ache, but it can range from mild and of no significance, to life-threatening. If you suspect any form of colic, you should consult your vet.

The main signs to look for are: your horse getting up and lying down repeatedly and rolling; standing and pawing the ground, or standing stretched out as if trying to urinate; and turning his head towards his flank and trying to kick his abdomen.

Always try to remove all your horse's food while waiting for the vet, and if he is rolling continuously, walk him around until the vet arrives.

What kinds of plants are poisonous to horses, and would they know to avoid them?

Some horses are like dogs and just eat anything, so it's always important to check your paddocks for poisonous plants. Common ones to look out for are bracken, acorns, deadly nightshade, hemlock, yew, rhododendron and ragwort.

Any plants should be dug up by their roots and removed.

 Ask Pippa

How can I tell if my horse is lame and what should I do about it?

Lameness is easiest to spot when the horse is trotting. If he's lame in front, when you trot him up he will raise his head when his sore leg hits the ground. If lame behind, he will tend to lean onto his sound side and also might drag the toe of his sore leg. Look for any obvious wounds, swellings or heat and check there is nothing stuck in his foot. If you think your horse is lame, you should stop riding him straightaway and consult a vet.

What is the best kind of bedding – straw or shavings?

We use straw bedding for all our youngsters. When they are weanlings we keep them in a barn on a deep-littered straw bed, and when they come in to be backed they are also kept on straw. A deep straw bed looks great and is cheaper than shavings.

All our competing horses are kept on shavings, mainly because this provides a dust free bed and they can't eat it! Shavings are also quicker to muck out than straw, which creates a bigger muck heap.

I don't think either is particularly better than the other, assuming they are both of good quality, and it is more about personal preference for you and your horse.

Do you have any tips for breaking in a horse?

This is a question I could write a whole book on! Briefly, if you are not experienced at backing youngsters I would strongly recommend you get someone who is to help you, or definitely get some good advice.

It's all about gaining your horse's confidence and trust. Take things slowly. Start by making sure your horse is happy with you handling him. Then see if he is comfortable wearing a rug, possibly with a surcingle (a strap which fastens about his girth area) so that he is used to the feeling of something round his tummy. After that, get him used to having a bit in his mouth and wearing a saddle.

When you're sure your horse is quite comfortable moving around with his tack on, and with his stirrups hanging down, you can start leaning over him.

Make sure the person helping you is confident and experienced handling young horses, and keep everything as calm as possible. Horses often get a bit worried when you first sit on them, so try to stay forward and then sit up slowly.

The most important piece of advice I can give you is just to take each step at a time, because all horses are different and some will take longer to back than others.

When is a sensible age to start breaking in my horse, and how long would you expect it to take?

We tend to break ours in during the autumn of their third year. It's best to do it before they get too big and strong! This is normally just basic handling, getting them used to the tack and trotting round the school with someone on. The process usually lasts four to six weeks and then they are turned out to grass for three to four months.

We bring them back in and repeat the same training when, having learned the basics, they take to being ridden much more easily. We take them out hacking, preferably with an older horse, who teaches them to go forwards and to enjoy their work.

But again, all horses are individuals, so there's no set time for each stage of their education. Bigger horses can often take longer because, despite their size, they might not be physically mature or strong enough to take too much work.

What's the best way to build a relationship with my horse to get the best out of him?

I strongly believe that horses should work for you because they want to, and not because they are being forced to. A horse needs to trust and respect you so that he is happy to do what you ask of him.

The best way to build a partnership with your horse is to spend time with him – not just riding him, but getting to know him in his stable. Grooming and general handling will also help. Always reward good behaviour, and if he is naughty make sure you stay calm but be firm.

Talk to your horse and watch his ears to see if he's interested and listening. Horses learn quickly to respond to voice commands as well as your other aids (see page 54).

Above all, remember that building a partnership is about building confidence together.

How can I get my nervous pony to trust me?

If you have a nervous pony, you'll need to spend a lot of time handling him so that he gets to know and trust you. Stay calm when you are around him, talk in a soft voice and try not to do anything in a rush, because horses can be frightened of unexpected or fast movements and loud voices.

Always reward your horse if he shows signs of improvement and sometimes just let him come to you and sniff you, rather than always going to him.

When you are riding, remember to keep calm and relaxed as he will pick up very quickly if you're nervous. As in the stable, speak to him in a quiet voice and don't be in a rush. Let him know through your body language that there's no reason for him to be anxious.

How would you go about putting a horse back into the field after box rest?

Horses and ponies naturally like to spend their time running free and grazing in fields, so box rest can cause a certain amount of stress. Unfortunately in some cases it is needed to help a horse recover from injuries, or conditions like laminitis.

To return a horse to pasture after box rest I would choose a nice, quiet day, preferably when there aren't too many flies around or, if it's winter, when the ground isn't too slippery.

If possible, start your horse off in a small paddock with a sensible horse in the field next to him, and keep a close eye on him. If you think it's necessary, you might want to get some sedalin paste or ACP tablets (mild sedatives) from your vet, which you can give your horse an hour before you want to turn him out.

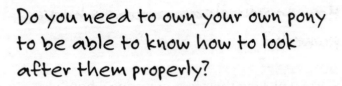

Do you need to own your own pony to be able to know how to look after them properly?

No, there are lots of riding schools where you can spend time with horses and ponies and learn how to look after and ride them.

I would strongly recommend that you learn as much as you can before you buy your own horse or pony. If you can't afford to go to a riding school you might be able to find a local yard where you can help out. The more hours you spend around ponies the more you will learn. And, as all horses and ponies are different, you will learn something new every day.

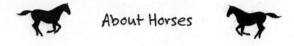

How do you clean a horse's hooves properly?

Start by picking their feet out using a hoof pick. You are removing any mud, bedding or stones in the underside of the hoof. This needs to be done daily, both before and after exercise, as stones can lead to a bruised foot and lameness.

Run your hand down the back of your horse's leg and squeeze above his fetlock joint. Then, holding the hoof in one hand, use the hoof pick to remove any muck, working from the heel towards the toe, avoiding the frog (the triangle in the middle of the hoof). After that, use a stiff brush to clean any mud away from the frog and then gently let the foot drop back down.

If the outside of the hooves needs cleaning too, you can use a wet stiff brush to clean them off and then when they are dry you can put some hoof oil on.

What advice would you give to someone looking for their first horse or pony?

The most important thing to remember is that owning any animal is a big commitment and responsibility. You must be absolutely sure you are thoroughly committed. When you're looking for your first horse or pony it's a good idea to ask a knowledgeable person, like your riding instructor, to help you find a horse that suits your lifestyle, needs and capabilities.

With your first horse, you should look for an older horse that has "been there, done that" and can help teach you.

Make sure that when you try him out you can handle him, tack him up and always watch someone else ride him first.

If it all looks good, try riding him in an enclosed space and afterwards, if you're happy, ask if someone can escort you out on a hack to make sure you can control him out of the school.

And always ask lots of questions about his medical history, shoeing, clipping, loading, whether he's good in traffic and if he has any vices.

Finally, when you think you've found the horse that's right for you, get your vet to give him the once-over to make sure he is up to the purpose you want him for.

 Ask Pippa

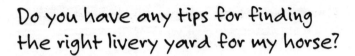

Do you have any tips for finding the right livery yard for my horse?

There are a lot of livery yards around, but it's always good to go for one that's been recommended to you by someone you trust.

First, you'll need to decide what sort of livery you want – whether it's do-it-yourself, part or full livery – and then look for a yard that can provide the service you require.

A good yard should have a knowledgeable person in charge who is willing to help, and I always prefer twenty-four-hour-care. You'll need to discuss the yard routine, bedding, feed, turn-out and make sure there is an alarmed and locked tack room.

As I said, the best thing to do is just to tell the yard what sort of service you'd like and see whether they can provide it. You'll also need to be prepared to pay the bills.

About Horses

How can I tell when my horse will need new shoes?

Our horses tend to be shod every four to six weeks, but it depends on what sort of work your horse is doing as to how long a set of shoes will last.

If a horse does a lot of road work, the shoes might wear out in about four weeks, but if he does a lot of school work he might go six weeks.

It is important to keep your horse well shod, because if his feet grow too long, his foot will become out of balance, which might lead to lameness. Remember the saying "no hoof, no horse".

Look out for missing, twisted or loose shoes, loose nails that push up from the wall of the hoof, or if the shoes are excessively thin, unevenly worn, or the hoof is starting to overgrow the shoe.

Why is clean tack so important?

You like to wear clean clothes, and your horse will appreciate clean tack, especially a clean bit in his mouth.

Clean tack will last longer. It's also essential to keep an eye on all the stitching on your tack. If the stitching goes on your stirrup leathers or girth while you are riding, you could have a serious accident.

We clean and check our tack every day. It's an important routine to establish.

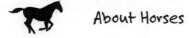

Why is grooming necessary?

This is another important routine. All our horses are groomed every day. Regular grooming keeps your horse healthy and comfortable, and helps you form a relationship with him.

Grooming cleans your horse and will prevent chafing under the tack. It also improves his coat and skin condition and allows you to keep an eye on his general health.

When you're grooming, always look out for any cuts, heat or swellings and check he hasn't got loose or missing shoes.

What equipment do I need to groom my horse?

Everybody has different grooming utensils and what you'll need depends on whether your horse is stabled, clipped out or turned out at grass.

A clipped horse is easy to groom – we use a hoof pick to do their feet, a large comb or hairbrush to brush their manes and tails, a soft body brush and metal curry comb (this is for cleaning the body brush not for use on your horse) to brush their body, and then to finish off, a warm, damp stable cloth on their head and body to remove any remaining grease.

If your horse lives out you will need a stiff dandy brush to remove the mud first and then use your body brush and metal curry comb. Another useful brush is a rubber curry comb, which is very good for removing loose hair.

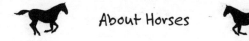

How do I plait my pony's mane or tail?

Plaiting is an art that needs plenty of practice!

To plait the mane you can use either a needle and thread, or elastic bands. I prefer it done with a needle and thread.

First, separate the mane into even sections and starting at the top of the neck, plait each section firmly down to the end and secure with thread or a rubber band. Then fold or roll each plait once or twice and secure it in the same way on top of the neck. You can plait the forelock in the same way.

For the best results on the tail, it needs to be full and untrimmed. Take even sections of hair from either side of the dock (the muscles and skin at the top of the tail) and keep the plait in the centre of the tail and as tight as possible. When you are nearly at the tip of the dock, finish the plait in the middle using the full length of the rest of the tail-hair (the skirt). Secure the end and fold the long plait under itself to the bottom of the dock and secure again.

How much space do I need to keep a horse?

This will vary depending on whether you have stables, or if your horse is outside all the time.

A competition horse that is stabled will need less room in a paddock as he has plenty of ridden exercise and so just needs to graze – about a quarter of an acre per horse would be fine.

Grass-kept horses need more room to run about and play, and they get most of their nutrition from the grass, so half an acre per horse would be ideal.

We have a stable, but no field to keep a horse. Will this be okay?

If you have a stable but no paddock, it's important to keep your horse well-exercised.

Maybe you could hand-graze your horse somewhere to break up his day. I am spoiled because I have a horse walker, so as well as being ridden every day, the horses also go on the walker.

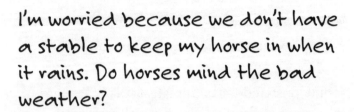

I'm worried because we don't have a stable to keep my horse in when it rains. Do horses mind the bad weather?

When it rains, you often see horses turn their bottoms towards the rain and try to shelter under a tree or by a hedge.

If you don't have a stable, you could provide your horse with a field shelter or make sure he has some trees or hedgerows to use. Horses cope very well with the cold because they tend to grow extra coat, but some do better if you put a well fitting New Zealand turn-out rug on them.

What kind of fencing would you recommend?

I think post-and-rail is the safest sort of fencing.

You could put some electric fencing on top of the post and rail, as this stops the horses chewing the rails, and also stops them fighting over the fence with a neighbour!

Remember to check regularly that, whatever fencing you have, it is safe and secure.

What's the best way to prepare my horse for travelling? Do I need any special equipment?

We use travelling boots or bandages on all four legs and a tail bandage or guard. The tail bandage will help prevent your horse rubbing his tail and the boots/bandages should prevent injury if he loses his balance or treads on himself during travelling.

If your horse hasn't travelled before, practise loading him in a lorry or trailer to make sure he is happy and confident with it. If he is reluctant to go in, a lunge line is a useful aid. Put it behind his quarters to help push him in.

Once inside, praise your horse and let him stand quietly in the lorry, preferably with some food.

Is it better to use a horsebox or a trailer?

I don't think it really matters whether you use a lorry or trailer. Some horses like to travel forwards in a lorry and others like to travel herringbone.

Just make sure that whatever method you use, the floor is safe and the transport is as light and airy as possible, and of course, that the vehicle is roadworthy.

How much should I feed my horse before a competition?

I give exactly the same as he normally eats.

Feed him at least an hour before travelling or working. We tend not to give our horses a hay-net on the way to a competition, unless they are competing later on in the day.

We've just moved house. What's the best way to help my pony settle into his new home?

Most ponies tend to settle into strange places very well but just keep an eye on him, and if he seems upset, maybe give him some hay to help keep him quiet and relax him.

If you are turning him out into a new field, stay with him for a while until he is settled. It is fairly normal for a horse or pony to gallop around in a strange field, so I would wait until he starts grazing or until he's quiet.

What makes a good field for a horse?

A good field should have safe fencing, an adequate supply of clean, fresh water and preferably some form of shelter from the wind, rain and the sun.

If your horse is kept on his own, it is quite nice if he can see some other animals. I prefer the field to be near enough for someone to be able to keep an eye on it, just in case he becomes distressed. And if the field is next to a road, I would be tempted to use a padlock and chain on the gate.

My friend clips her horse during the winter, but then puts a rug on him anyway to keep him warm. What's the point?

We clip our horses in the winter because they naturally grow a thicker coat, so clipping stops them sweating so much when you work them. They also take a long time to dry if they have a long coat and they're much more likely to get chills and lose condition quickly.

But after you've clipped a horse, you also need to make sure he's warm enough when he's not working. A rug replaces the coat that he has lost. It's also a lot easier to keep your horse clean when he is clipped.

What's the easiest way to go about bringing my pony in from the field?

Take a small titbit with you in your pocket. Call your pony's name to get his attention, then confidently but quietly walk towards his shoulder. Place his head collar on first and then give him his treat.

As you lead him in, stay close to his nearside shoulder. If there are other horses in the field make sure that when you shut the gate you stay by his shoulder to avoid any accident.

ABOUT RIDING

Ask Pippa

What's the secret to being a great rider?

I do not think there is any secret to being a great rider but I do know there is an awful lot of hard work over many years.

You need some luck for sure, and obviously you need horse power. The best rider in the world cannot go to a championship without a good horse, but the art is in producing that good horse, nurturing it over the years.

I believe great riders can achieve on many different horses and it's not just about being able to ride well. It's about the whole aspect of horsemanship, working out how each individual horse thinks, and working with them, not against them.

What's your top riding tip?

My top tip would probably be to keep things simple – concentrate more on yourself and improving your own balance, rather than worrying about correcting your horse. Riding is all about balance.

Ruth McMullen, to whom I owe much of my success, always used to say to me that eighty-five per cent of horses' problems are caused by what the rider is doing on top. I have to mention one other tip, and that would be patience. There are no shortcuts.

What does my riding instructor mean when she talks about using "aids"?

Your legs, hands, seat, back and voice are all aids. They are called aids because they aid/help you to ride your horse.

If you are in correct balance, you should be able to use them simultaneously or independently. If your instructor says you are using conflicting aids, it means you are asking one thing with one set of aids and telling your horse to do the opposite with another set. For example, you might ask him to go forward with your legs but your hands are not allowing him to.

Whips and spurs are known as artificial aids.

Why is warming up so important?

Like any human athlete, warming up is very important.

You are getting your horse to relax and quietly loosen up by gently stretching his muscles, before asking him to physically work harder. This will help prevent cramping and muscle fatigue, and also it really helps the horse mentally.

It's just as important to cool down too – by this I mean letting your horse stretch his muscles and loosen off at the end of his work on a long rein.

So you have a crescendo effect building up to the more demanding exercises, then the easing off period after your main work.

How can I stop my horse being so aggressive on the lunge?

Lunging, if done correctly, can be highly beneficial to a horse, and he shouldn't be aggressive.

Often when lunged my horses can think 'Yippee!' and have a buck and a play at the beginning of the session, which I don't have a problem with. But if your horse is rude and aggressive he obviously needs quietly disciplining. Bring him to a walk and begin the exercise again until he is listening to what you are asking him to do.

It would help to have a confined area to lunge him in – a lunge pen ideally. If you don't have one of these you could make a temporary area using some jump wings and poles.

Make sure you have the correct tack. I would use a normal bridle without the reins, or a lunge cavesson, then I'd use either side reins or running reins attached to the saddle or a special roller and a decent lunge rein and a whip.

Remember the triangle rule – your horse being one edge, the lunge rein being another and the lunge whip being the third edge. Try as hard as you can to stay in the middle, lunging the horse around you.

Keeping him on a fairly small circle to start with (that way you will have more control if he starts to get aggressive), make him do a transition to walk using a very positive voice, and then reward with the same voice when he reacts in the right way. Continue repeating walk, trot, trot, walk transitions, making him come to a standstill at times too, then hopefully you will be able to progress from there.

What's the most important thing to remember when I'm learning to jump?

Confidence – both yours and your horse's. It's always better to work on perfecting your own balance and position, and to work on the quality of your horse's canter and rhythm over poles and small fences, than just seeing how big you can jump.

How long does it take to train a horse?

Many years, but just one day can make a difference too. I never stop training my horses. Like us, they never stop learning. It's on-going, but very rewarding.

I would like to start doing some lateral work on my pony. Could you tell me how I should go about it?

Once your horse or pony has established the basics on the flat and is accepting your aids, it's fun and very helpful to start incorporating some lateral work.

I begin by experimenting, quietly moving them away from one leg or the other. By this I mean pushing your horse perhaps three or four strides away from the left leg so he takes a few sideways steps from left to right. Then, when he gets the hang of that, I'll push him away from the right leg moving from right to left.

Keep it simple at this stage. Just get your horse's head as straight as possible, then try a few steps away from the edge of the school or even riding up a quiet lane, followed by a few steps back. I always start all my lateral work in walk, once the horse understands what you are asking then you can try it in a faster pace.

Once he understands moving away from one leg
or the other you will then find it easier to
progress to 'shoulder-in', where your horse's feet
are on three different tracks, with his inside
foreleg on one track, his inside hind leg on the
same track as his outside foreleg, his outside
hind on the third track. You should aim to have a
small amount of bend to the inside.

Rather than thinking about pace, the correct
bend, the correct angle and everything else right
from the beginning, just try to concentrate on
keeping the same, consistent angle.

Top tips to remember – don't collapse your hips
when you are using one leg or the other. It will
help you to stay riding on a straight line if you
keep looking up and ahead in the direction you
want to go. Always allow your horse to go
forward, as it can be very easy to block and
restrict the forward movement by tightening
your arms.

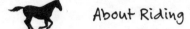 About Riding

Is it okay to ride a horse that has not been shod?

We start all of our young horses without shoes – we're lucky because we have good surfaces. Later, we have them shod in front, but from a safety point of view we don't shoe any of them behind while they are being broken in.

I have heard of cases where people ride horses that aren't shod – but they must be very restricted as to where they ride and what they can do with their horses. I know only too well how much a horse can slip when going cross country if he's pulled a shoe off on the course. You suddenly have no shoe and no studs and a sore foot at the end of the round!

So I think it's always safer, for both horse and rider, for the horse to be well shod.

What's the difference between galloping, cantering and trotting?

Galloping is faster than cantering and the horse's foot fall is different too. Galloping is four-beat, the same as walk. In other words, the horse places each foot down on the ground at different times. If you see a horse with a good ground covering walk, it is a good indication that the horse can gallop well, which is what we look for in eventing.

Cantering is slower than galloping, but faster than trotting. Cantering is three-beat. If your horse is in left canter, he leads with the right hind leg, and the left hind leg and right forelegs work together, followed by the left foreleg.

Trotting, by contrast, is two-beat, because the opposite hind leg is placed on the ground at the same time as the opposite front leg, so the left fore and right hind move at the same time, followed by the right fore and the left hind.

I'm worried about riding on the road. How can I make sure I'm safe?

It is sensible to be concerned about riding on the roads because it is obviously potentially dangerous. But you can minimise a lot of the risks.

First of all, make sure you are visible, and try to avoid riding in poor light.

I always prefer to go out with a companion, particularly if I'm riding a younger horse or one that's worried by traffic. And whether it's correct or not I like to ride two abreast if possible because I feel cars seem to slow down more.

Concentrate at all times and be aware of your surroundings and what's ahead of you. If there's a car coming and you can see something scary ahead (a plastic bag at the edge of the road, for example), then either wait and signal the car to pass before you get to the spooky object, or signal for the car to stop while you pass.

Likewise if a lorry comes from behind, I would always signal him to slow right down and trot to the nearest drive/gateway, unless my horse was absolutely bomb proof in traffic. If a lorry approaches from the front I will often signal them to stop while I go past, or again I will find a driveway or somewhere to get off the road.

Remember, if you feel your horse really is too naughty or you have not got enough control, do not jeopardise yours or other road users' safety as well as your horse's by going out on the road. I am lucky because, with the odd very sharp horse which can whip round quickly, I can take him down a quiet lane and onto a bridle path.

Finally, always, always use plenty of hand signals and remember to acknowledge and thank drivers for slowing down. After all, why should they be courteous to us if we aren't courteous to them?

What does it mean if a horse is wearing a red ribbon on its tail?

A red ribbon on a horse's tail warns people not to get too close to his rear end in case he kicks. A green ribbon warns you that he's a young horse and could be unpredictable, so again it's wise not to get too close.

How can I tell if my horse's saddle fits correctly?

You can definitely tell if you have an incorrectly fitting saddle because your horse will be sore.

A correctly fitting saddle should not come too low over the horse's withers, and it should not put pressure on any point of his spine. It should sit evenly on the horse so that when the rider is on, the pressure from the seat is well spread. I would first put the saddle on your horse without a numnah because you'll be able to see more clearly whether it fits properly.

I also like to stand back and look to see if the rider will naturally sit in the centre. You can tell by looking at the seat whether the rider might be tipped too far forward or tipped backwards. There are numnahs and various pads you can get that will help with this.

I have lots of different shaped horses, and with eventing they change shape throughout the year. In January they come in nice and porky, but by their major three-day events, they are fitter and carrying less weight. I couldn't possibly have a saddle or two for every horse, so I use polypads with a riser pad with my dressage saddle, and a numnah with a half-sheepskin pad for my jumping saddles.

I'm certainly not an expert in this field, but if I have any concerns I will ask my saddle manufacturer, and likewise I would suggest you ask for advice if you're not sure. It's hard enough to sit in true balance without being hindered by an incorrectly fitting saddle!

What about the rest of the tack?

It's always vitally important that any of the tack put on our horses fits correctly so they are comfortable and the tack has the effect it's supposed to. Badly fitting tack not only causes discomfort, skin abrasions and sores, but also makes horses difficult to control – because it's only natural for them to resist and run away from pain.

A horse's mouth is extremely sensitive so the bit must be the correct width for his mouth, and not sit too low, because it will clink on his teeth and allow him to get his tongue over. Likewise if too high it will be very uncomfortable.

Nosebands should fit according to their purpose. Flash and cavessons sit just below the horse's cheekbones. The top strap of the flash should be fairly tight so that when the bottom strap is done up it doesn't pull the top part any lower on the nose. The drop should sit lower but still remain on the bony part of his nose. A grackle noseband is sold either as a normal grackle or a high-fitting grackle, I prefer the latter where the rings on the grackle have sheepskin underneath, and again for comfort sit higher up on the cheek. Grackles are especially good used along with gags and bits that have upward leverage, because they avoid pinching.

Headpieces, browbands and cheekpieces should fit according to the size of your horse's head. Personally I always like to be able to adjust a bridle so that I am not on the top or bottom holes of all the buckles. This applies to all tack, especially girths, as if you're on the top hole each side and your horse loses a bit of weight or runs up, then your saddle will slip.

Martingales and breastplates must not be too tight and restricting, which will cause your horse to come against it. Likewise, if they are too big and loopy they will have no effect and could potentially be very dangerous when jumping because your horse might get a front leg caught in them. I'd advise a breastplate to be used with any saddle that slips back.

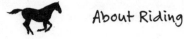

What is a half halt? How do I get my horse to do it?

A half halt is the expression used when we want to balance our horse by making him think he is being asked to stop but keeping pressure on with the leg so his hind legs stay active and you don't actually stop. It has the effect of sitting/rocking him back, like a seesaw, so he lowers and engages (works harder) with his hind legs. This enables him to lighten his front end so he can be in self carriage (i.e. in a better shape to move forward effectively). Remember, the horse's power comes from his back end.

Another term I like to use is "ride a dummy transition". You pretend you're going to make a downward transition and get your horse really waiting for you, then send him forwards again. It's great to help balance him and very useful for horses that anticipate.

I love riding, but I don't own a horse. Can I still join the Pony Club?

Anyone under the age of twenty-one can become a member of the Pony Club, but if you don't own your own pony or horse, rather than joining a branch, you could join one of the Pony Club's special centres, where they have horses and ponies you can ride. Visit the Pony Club website for more details and to find out where your nearest centre is.

I would encourage any young enthusiast to join. Like many of my fellow team mates, I came up through the Pony Club. It's a wonderful organisation that really teaches the all-round basics of riding and horse management. You never stop learning, but more importantly, you'll meet lots of people and have loads of fun.

My riding teacher suggested I get my horse some over-reach boots. What do they do?

Over-reach boots are used to prevent your horse from over-reaching, which is when his hind foot steps on the heal of his front foot. This can sometimes be very nasty. Over-reaches happen more often when jumping, particularly when going cross-country and often when the ground is wet and muddy. I always run mine cross-country in over-reach boots.

Make sure they fit correctly and aren't too big. I would also use them when I lunge, especially with horses I know might have a buck and a play, or if I think one is going to be particularly excited when turned out.

I fell off my horse recently and hurt myself quite badly. Now I'm frightened to ride. How can I get my confidence back?

It is never nice falling off and even worse if you hurt yourself. But one thing you can always be sure of as a rider is that we are all going to fall off at some stage. I definitely find there is truth in the saying that "the older you get the less you bounce"!

Providing you haven't hurt yourself very badly, I think it is very important that you get straight back on, because the longer you wait, the more time you have to dwell on it. I find if I fall off I am either angry with myself for coming off in the first place so I want to get back on immediately, or else the horse has been naughty or green so I have to get straight back on to resolve the problem.

If you have a nastier fall and you are injured, then make sure you give yourself enough time to recover physically before getting back on. If you are very nervous and feel as though you've lost your confidence, take small steps. Get back on a sensible, reliable horse or pony that you trust, and don't push yourself too hard. As the days go by and you find yourself growing more confident, you can start to slowly push yourself a little bit more each time you ride. Remember, we all want to enjoy our riding at whatever level.

It's the same when horses lose their confidence with jumping – take your horse back to basics, starting over poles and small fences and work on jumping them correctly.

Finally I'd say that the key thing about getting back on is to try not to think too much, and don't let your imagination play tricks on you. Accidents happen and it doesn't mean you're a bad rider or that your horse is necessarily naughty.

My horse is sometimes backward thinking. I can feel he is going to stop, but the more pressure I apply, the more he resists. What can I do to overcome this?

Some horses can be more backward thinking than others. I think the main thing to work on is getting them really responsive to the leg, so they learn when you ask them to move forward with your leg that they have to respond instantly, not a second, or even half a second later. Lots and lots of repeated transitions will help. Training your horse to listen to your leg means that as soon as you even sense or feel him thinking backwards you can give him a quick nudge of encouragement forward, without giving him time to pull up or stop.

Very often a horse takes advantage because we have missed or ignored the early signs of him dropping behind the leg or ignoring the fact that he has slightly hung towards home or his friends. Even if you sense this only slightly, remind him you're there and send him forward off the leg. If he has gone even further down the line and is napping, then don't jeopardise your safety. Lead him to a suitable, safe environment where you can overcome the problem. Don't be afraid if he really needs kicking, you might need to kick him hard to get him to listen. It's much safer than trying to resolve the problem on concrete or tarmac where he could potentially lose his footing and slip over.

My pony won't strike on the right leg when cantering on the right rein. What can I do?

Often a horse will strike off on the wrong leg into canter if he is not straight and upright. With the right rein, a common problem is that when a rider asks for the canter transition, they tip forward and to the inside, taking away the outside leg. This causes the horse to lose his straightness, his shoulders fall out, and he moves to the left so he strikes off in left canter.

To avoid this, when you ask for the canter, make sure your horse is in front of your leg so you know he is going to react instantly off your leg as you ask for the transition. Stay very tall, keep the outside rein and leg on, and slightly raise the inside hand, so you have a small bit of bend to the left. This gives room for him to strike off from his right shoulder, but don't let him fall out as you ask and keep looking up (thinking of keeping your left, or outside, shoulder down will stop you from tipping in).

When I have my horse going forward, he will go onto the bit and lose his shape through the corners. How do I sustain his shape?

I often try to think of balancing my horses before each corner, so that through the turn I can just let them move forward. I prepare and set up for each corner knowing that I want the horse to gain impulsion through each turn so that he stays connected and remains in the correct outline. I use my inside leg before to create the bend through his body, and then the outside leg to bring him around and keep in shape.

How do you get a horse's head in while it is leaning on the bit?

It's not a case of getting your horse's head in while he is leaning on the bit that you should be focused on.

Instead, you need to work on getting your horse sitting behind so that he takes his weight onto his hind legs and can lighten and take his weight off his forehand. I think of the horse as being like a seesaw – I want him to tip onto his back end so the front end lifts. As soon as this happens, he'll stop leaning and you can think about riding him forward with a light contact, rather than feeling you are doing a lot of pulling to try and get him rounder using just your hands. Again lots of repeated downward transitions and half halts will help you to get your horse to sit, take the weight behind and engage.

Remember he has to carry himself, and if he is leaning you are obviously carrying him.

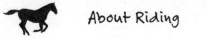

About Riding

Why is it hard to kick in rising trot?

Maybe you are struggling to keep your balance.

Remember to ride with a secure lower leg wrapped snugly round your horse or pony with a soft knee. If you find you need to give a kick, do it when your seat is in the saddle, on the down part of the up-down rising trot.

I find it hard to stay in the saddle when doing double and triple jumps. Can you give me any advice?

You need to work on improving your balance when jumping.

It's difficult to answer without seeing what you are doing, but it sounds as though you lose your balance over a fence and you take time to get it back. When jumping a single fence, you obviously have the time to get it back, but with a double or triple you only have one or two strides.

Whenever you jump, really concentrate on your lower leg position, keeping your heel down. On the approach, take off, in the air, landing and move off, don't let that lower leg move.

The most common fault is when we grip and pivot with our knees and allow the lower leg to slip back. Then we get in front of the movement and lose our balance forwards, or our legs go too far forward and we lose our balance backwards.

So focus on your legs and staying tall right up until the point of take off, and as soon as you land, sit up.

Be very strict with yourself and start by perfecting your position over small fences, incorporating combination fences, before progressing to the bigger jumps.

My pony is lazy. When my mum rides him, he goes nicely for her, but when I ride him, he stops because my legs aren't as long as my mum's so I can't keep him going. How can I get him to go better for me?

I am afraid a lot of it comes down to you getting stronger and more effective with your legs, and it's easier said than done. If your pony is very lazy and doesn't respond to your legs, a pair of spurs will help. But try to avoid endless nagging with your legs – it's much more effective to give a couple of good firm kicks, and if he doesn't listen to that, tickle him with your stick. Remember, you're the boss, not him.

My pony is scared of noisy show grounds. How can I get him used to the different noises so that I can do some indoor shows this winter?

The only way to get your pony used to all the noises and distractions of a show ground is to keep taking him to them, even if it's just to ride around and not actually compete so he doesn't feel the pressure of having to perform and can just get used to the atmosphere.

I've also heard of people making recordings of clapping and different noises to play at home in the yard so the horses get used to the sounds. One of mine is terrified of flapping flags and I have put a flag outside his stable so that he gets used to it and realises there is nothing to worry about.

Remember to stay patient and calm. On the whole your pony is probably genuinely worried, not being naughty or disobedient, so getting cross with him will only make the situation worse.

I have trouble controlling my horse because I'm not strong enough. Do you have any tips?

Controlling your horse is not always about strength. It's about training and using feel instead of force. For sure some big, strong horses might be unsuitable for a girl, but that's why it's so important when trying a horse or pony to find an appropriate type.

Stay sitting up. If your horse pulls you forward, you end up pulling and tugging with the hands, it's much more effective to use your seat and back to help hold him. The more you pull, the more he will pull back.

If you sense your horse is about to quicken his pace, make a small correction immediately. All too often we wait too long or miss the early signs of a horse losing his balance and straightness, we don't make little corrections early enough and we end up having to make a major correction later, which involves more physical strength.

When I canter I find it hard not to bounce all over the place. How can I get better at sitting properly?

I often have days when I concentrate solely on my own position and balance.

I find having a neck strap or a strap fixed across the front of the saddle to hold onto can really help. Riding without stirrups will also help you to improve. Make sure you're not tempted to grip with your thighs and knees in order to keep your balance. Keep your legs long, loose and relaxed.

Look up, make sure you grow tall, stretch your tummy muscles and have your shoulder, hip and heel in a straight line and try to go with the horse's movement and feel as if you are just an extension of your horse.

My pony often walks deliberately slowly when I'm leading him back to the stables after a lesson. How can I stop him doing this?

Make sure that you stay by your pony's shoulder when leading, and don't be tempted to pull him along. You could try having a long dressage stick in your left hand to help encourage him forward, clicking at the same time so he associates the click with forward movement, and keeping him as straight as you can.

Or it might be that you need someone else on the ground to help. They could either walk on the other side or slightly behind to encourage him forward, but obviously at a safe enough distance not to be on the receiving end of a kick or a buck.

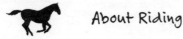
Whenever I lead my horse, she nips me. What can I do to stop this?

I would be inclined to just give a little short, sharp tug on the rein or rope with my right hand as soon as they try to nip and I would probably use my voice and say "no" firmly at the same time.

If that didn't work, I'd hold a short stick or cane in my right hand, gripping it a little lower down the stick than you would normally. Then, when she goes to nip, you can give her a little light tap, or she will end up nipping the stick before your hand.

During riding lessons, my instructor always tells me to give my pony a good smack with the whip because he's stubborn, but I'm worried I'm hurting him. What should I do?

Sticks, whips and spurs are what we call artificial aids. They are used to back up other aids, particularly our leg aids.

We have to work hard to train our horses to respond to a light leg aid, and if they don't, they get a good sharp kick with the heel, and if they ignore that, a flick with a stick.

I know it is easier said than done, and I'm well aware some ponies can be a bit stubborn and take advantage of the fact their young jockeys might lack physical strength. But that's all the more reason to have a small pair of spurs, or carry a dressage whip to help send your pony forward and avoid endlessly nag, nag, nagging him with an ineffective leg.

About Riding

Your pony has to learn than you are in charge
and if you ask him to go forward, that means go
forward. He will gradually become more
responsive providing you are always consistent. A
flick with your whip will not hurt him, but it will
encourage him to respond to what you're asking.

My pony spooks around certain other ponies. How can I help him with this?

Some ponies and horses are more horse-shy than others. We've found this with a few of our homebreds, and I'm sure it's because as youngsters they are brought up in a herd environment, where ten to fifteen are turned out together. It's natural instinct for them to develop a pecking order. As you can imagine, in excess of ten unruly yearlings and two- year-olds all playing, galloping, and bucking, they learn to dodge each other's flying hooves!

With the horse-shy ones, at competitions I will try to find a quiet area or corner so that I don't have too many other horses getting in the way. You do have to be more vigilant when riding, and try to avoid going directly towards an oncoming horse.

Turn away or make a change of direction if possible, otherwise I transition down, slow the pace and warn other riders that my horse is nervous of others and they will have to be considerate.

Over time I've found they do improve and get more confident, but remember your pony isn't being naughty, so you need to deal with it in a way that will help build his confidence.

When my pony bucks, I always fall off no matter how hard I try to stay on. How can I stop this from happening?

It can be very difficult staying on a pony that bucks. The safest thing to do if your pony goes to buck is to kick him forward and use your reins to get his head up. It's when his head goes right down and he drops his shoulders and stops that we come off, because our balance gets shifted forward.

No matter what happens stick your legs right forward and get your upper body back, lean back slightly if you have to. A neck strap will help as well, so hold onto that as you sit back and kick. He will struggle to get you off if you are not tipped out of forward balance.

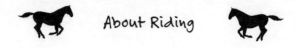

Why does my horse rear, and what should I do when it happens?

Rearing is a major problem, which must be dealt with immediately before it turns into a potentially very dangerous habit.

The key is not to allow horses to rear in the first place. As much as possible I try to avoid putting an unestablished green youngster into a situation where he could potentially rear or nap before he has learned to respond quickly to the leg aid.

Many of the answers to these questions are the same, it comes down to horses truly accepting the leg. Whatever they see, whatever is going on around them, they still have to understand that as soon as you ask them to go forward or to move away from the leg, they have to respond instantly.

If your horse rears you must make sure you get your balance well forward. If you lose your balance backwards, which can easily happen when a horse is standing up, you risk pulling him over backwards, or else he may lose his balance, resulting in both horse and rider having a very nasty fall. It might be useful to have someone on the ground with a lunge whip to help you send the horse forward. Remember, horses cannot stand up if they are going forward.

Finally I would suggest you get advice from someone with plenty of experience to overcome this habit. REMEMBER, NEVER JEOPARDISE YOUR OWN SAFETY.

My horse hates water ditches. How can I reassure him that they are okay?

One of the bonuses of producing your own horses is that you know exactly what has happened in their past. So, if you have a problem with a horse not liking water ditches you know whether he has had a frightening experience to cause it, and you'll be able to tell if he is being naughty or if he is genuinely worried.

But no matter what, you have to try everything to overcome the problem.

As part of their education all our young horses routinely get used to popping over little plastic water trays as well as spooky little fillers, all very small. I try to make them obey that golden rule of staying straight and in front of the leg. I never use speed to get over to the other side. I want them to look and see what they are being asked to do and I will keep repeating the exercise until they feel confident. Once I feel they are sufficiently off my aids I will take them cross-country schooling or go and find some small hazards such as little ditches out hacking, I will always take an experienced horse to give the younger one a lead. You must start small with a diddy little ditch and only progress when your horse is feeling happy and confident. I have only had a handful of horses over the years that have said no to a ditch, and more often than not they have stopped, and then the issue becomes more in their heads and trying to evade you as a rider rather than with the ditch itself.

Perseverance is the key. If the horse flatly says "no", I'll keep nudging him forward. If he whips around, I will turn him back again, trying everything to not let him turn again. A lot of patience and encouragement is needed, so don't put a time scale on it.

Eventually, when your horse realises you're not going to give in, he will give into you. If you let him off and walk home without resolving the situation I can guarantee he will keep taking advantage.

Primmore's Pride, one of my best horses, did exactly this. It took me two hours to get him over his first ever ditch. It was only a foot wide and six inches deep, but after that he never looked at another ditch, and we never had another confrontation.

Finally, if, even with training, my horses remain worried about ditches, or I feel they are not suitably brave enough for cross country, I will find another job for them.

How do I "use more leg"?

Once the horse learns to listen and respond to the leg you won't need to use loads and loads of leg.

The key is to make sure that whenever you use it, you get a response. If you don't get a response from a light leg aid, kick him harder and keep kicking him until he does respond and listen.

Remember, you nudge with the leg or kick with the heel to get him to move forwards or away from it. Then you have the holding, moulding leg, where you snuggle his sides with your inner calves to create more bend through his middle piece. I find this is the part of the leg that talks and gives him confidence, and you close it for the downward transitions.

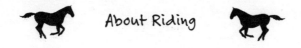
How can I get my horse to canter more slowly when approaching jumps?

It's back to flat work again. For your horse to canter more slowly into his fences, he has to improve his balance and self carriage, and for this he needs more engagement from behind. You can help him with this by working lots on the different canters – collected, working, and building up to medium canter, with lots of transitions within the pace as well, trot/canter, canter/trot, then walk/canter, canter/walk.

A helpful exercise is to introduce four canter poles set nine metres apart, and work on keeping the same pace and rhythm between them. When your horse is relaxed, you can incorporate a jump, but the canter poles should help you to sit more still on the last four strides and they will help your horse to keep the same stride length and speed you require.

Rome wasn't built in a day, and doing the correct work regularly will help you and your horse to gradually find it easier and easier.

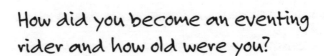

How did you become an eventing rider and how old were you?

I suppose when I was younger I dreamed of riding at Badminton, and I was inspired when I read Lucinda Green's book, *Up, Up and Away*. I loved hunting too, it was such fun getting covered in mud, jumping ditches and hedges, going through streams. I also enjoyed taking part in hunter trials during the Easter holidays. Back then I didn't really understand dressage, so I found it boring. Standing in line, normally down at the bottom end in the show ring, didn't appeal either.

The deciding factor was when I got my first horse, Sir Barnaby, who was owned by Ruth McMullen, a well-respected horse trainer (who still trains me thirty years on!). It was Ruth who taught me and made me understand the importance of flat work, and Barnaby who took me from Pony Club eventing teams to Badminton.

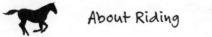

Eventing is an expensive sport. How can someone starting out get good rides? Any tips or advice would be helpful.

I fully understand how expensive eventing is and what a hard struggle it can be for many, including me.

I was very lucky because I served an apprenticeship for eight years with Ruth McMullen. I learned an incredible amount from her, and she gave me the opportunity to ride an amazing number of very different horses – from eventers to show ponies, racehorses to Arabs. She had a name and a very good reputation, so people from all areas used to send horses and ponies to her for breaking and training. This gave me so much experience of riding different shapes and sizes, some with talent, but many without. Our job was to educate and improve them all.

Unless you are very fortunate and have an open cheque book, I don't think many people start out with a lot of good rides. I am not sure if this is good advice, but try hard to go wherever you can go, ride whatever horse or pony you can ride and seize every opportunity that comes your way.

Be prepared to work exceedingly hard, be honest to the horses you ride and to yourself. There isn't really a clear path through, but hopefully if you are determined enough to succeed and have a bit of natural talent you will get noticed – and of course some luck thrown in would be useful as well!

What's the best way to prepare for a competition and get as much experience as possible?

In a way you have answered your own question. The best way to prepare is for you and your horse to get as much experience as possible before you compete.

It's important to make a good plan for any competition. First, find the right competition which suits you and your horse's capabilities, in whatever equestrian discipline you choose. There is no point in entering something neither of you is ready for. It will only set you back, and it will certainly not help either your confidence or your horse's. You must make sure you are both fit enough for the competition planned, and for eventing that is an absolute necessity .

I always think that I am better off being over prepared than under prepared, and I try to leave no stone unturned. Arriving at a competition knowing I have done everything possible makes me feel positive. I don't want to see a course and wish I'd prepared more at home.

With dressage tests I will make sure I know what the tests are at least the week before. I give myself plenty of time to get really familiar with the test and ride through the movements. There is enough to think about when riding a test at a competition, so it helps enormously not to have to worry about where I'm going.

With my young horses I will have them working above the level I am expecting them to compete at, so that when they go to their first small competition they can still cope with everything that is being asked of them. If I was asking them to deal with distractions and bigger jumps than they'd seen before, I'd be asking for trouble!

Tip – remember, part of your planning is to have all the correct tack and gear with you, in particular your horse. Believe it or not, that happened to me once – I went to a show and one of the horses I was meant to be riding had been left at home!

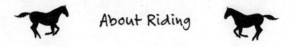

What do all the different coloured rosettes mean in eventing?

Very often events are sponsored so the rosettes can often be the same colour. Otherwise it is typically red for first, blue for second then it seems to vary from event to event. I prefer the red and blue ones myself!!

Ask Pippa

What exactly is "dressage"?

Dressage is a French word most commonly translated as "training". The art of riding and training a horse in a manner that develops obedience, flexibility and balance. This is why, whatever equestrian discipline we choose, dressage builds those solid foundations, training our horses to respond to our body signals.

I'm really nervous about my first showjumping event. Do you have any tips?

Be well prepared (see page 103).

Remember, many of us suffer from nerves, so it's about learning to control them and turning negative thoughts into positive ones, sometimes easier said than done. I try not to let my mind play tricks on me, often the imagination works over time. I don't let it – I make myself think of something else. Rather than thinking in negatives, "I must not do this or that", I think "I must do this or that". It keeps me more positively focused.

And always remember we do this because we love the sport, we don't do it to torment ourselves!

When I showjump, why do I have to lean forward?

It is not so much about leaning forward when you jump, it's about keeping your balance and going with the horse's movement. If you think too much about leaning forward when you jump you could easily get in front of your horse, causing him to throw his weight too much onto his forehand/shoulders.

If you concentrate on keeping your lower leg in the correct position on the approach, take off, over the fence, on landing and departure, and sitting as still as possible, it should help. I like to think of sitting tall as well, right to the point where the horse leaves the ground, then I allow myself to follow the movement keeping my legs connected. If you grip and pivot on your knee the lower leg will slip too far back, become ineffective and your body will go too far forward.

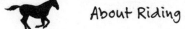

How long should your stirrups be for jumping?

The length will vary from person to person, but whatever length makes it easier to keep your balance and enable you to go with the horse's movement.

I find my length can slightly vary from horse to horse too. I would go up about six holes from my dressage length to my showjumping length, and up another two or three from my showjumping length for my cross-country length.

I think if you ride too short it is easier to loose your balance forward, too long your balance backwards.

My horse overreaches when I go cross-country. I put overreach boots on her, but she pulls her back shoes off too. How can I stop this happening?

I always go cross-country in correctly fitting over-reach boots. They must not be too large. If you find your horse is regularly pulling off shoes when you go cross-country it might be worth speaking to your farrier to see if he could shoe him slightly differently, maybe just a touch shorter so the back of the shoe doesn't stick out quite so far. It's quite uncommon for a horse to be regularly pulling off hind shoes, again speak to your farrier and see what he suggests. If she is pulling off her hind shoes by stepping on them with the other hind foot you could try a sausage boot, which goes around the pastern, particularly if she moves very close behind.

What is a dog-leg fence?

There is not a fence called a dog-leg fence, but you have a dog-leg turn or bend because it is shaped like the hind leg of a dog. So you have fences on a dog leg, where you land over one fence and have a dog-leg turn to another.

I would love to be a professional eventer. How can I step up a level?

To be a professional in any sport is tough, but I think ours could well be one of the toughest.

I know any sport has its ups and downs but I find eventing can be emotionally draining. The partnerships created can be incredibly special and that is the part that I find the hardest. I am constantly beating myself up when I feel I am letting my horses down, or when they suffer injuries.

The constant pressure of making ends meet in what is becoming an ever increasingly expensive sport is tough (hence in my spare time, which I guarantee I don't have much of, I write books!). Having said that, being a professional, it really is the most wonderful sport, which many of us become addicted to. This is why Mark Todd and Blyth Tait have returned to it having been retired for some years, and why many of us are still competing and running large strings in our forties.

To start with it is trying to make a name for yourself, whether this is getting good results on a horse or couple of horses, or taking in young ones for schooling and offering a service to people. If you do a good job with the horses you'll hopefully get recommended to others. It is not just about riding, it's about getting owners, or attracting owners would be a better espression. Owners are the most important ingredient of a professional rider.

So why should an owner send a horse to you instead of another professional? Many riders find it easy to sell themselves to owners, but if you are like me it's difficult to blow your own trumpet, so you try to sell what you are good at selling. In my case I've had a lot of experience in producing young horses, so people send me young horses to break and school and from there I've been able to persuade them to leave the horses with me to start eventing. I have always sold the fact that the attention to detail I provide, particularly from a management point of view, and the one-to-one care the horses are given, is second to none. My owners know that their horses are not one of a number, they are all individuals, none of whom go short of attention, care and love. Maybe I am just soppy but that would be important to me and so it is to owners too.

Do as good a job as you possibly can, let your owners know your thoughts, where you think their horse's strengths and weaknesses are, involve them in where you should, or shouldn't, take their horses. Look after your owners and don't give them a reason to send their horse somewhere else. I am well aware that without my owners I would not have been able to follow my dreams and goals.

As for stepping up a level, that is down to hard work, when you are ready and, above all, when your horses are ready. Always remember, no matter what we might want, our judgement must never be clouded. The most important question to ask is, "Is the horse ready or up for the task?" His interests and welfare are more important than anything else.

ABOUT
PIPPA

 Ask Pippa

What was the name of your first pony or horse?

My first pony was a little black pony called Pepsi. We did all the local shows together in the summer, and during winter I rode him from the field. He lived out and had a very woolly coat and was often covered in mud. When brushing the mud off him, I used to dream about one day having a clipped horse who lived in a stable during the winter.

Do you have a favourite horse, and why?

I try not to have favourites but obviously there have been some special horses over the years.

Sir Barnaby was my first horse, who took me from the Pony Club to competing at Badminton and Burghley.

Bits and Pieces, the little coloured horse who defied all the rules, wasn't designed to compete at the level he did, but he was placed both at Badminton and Burghley. He was the horse that got me my first Union Jack, the first one I rode to represent the country at senior championship level.

Supreme Rock will always be very dear to my heart. So many people told me to give up with him, but we went on to win two Badmintons and two European Championships. He also took me to my first Olympics, where we were part of the silver medal team.

Primmore's Pride was a very tall, narrow horse who won the three big four-star events, two of which were part of the Rolex Grand Slam.
At present, Redesigned, Mirage D'elle and Billy Landretti . . . I think the list could go on and on, let me say I love them all.

How many horses and ponies have you ridden?

I can't answer this one, because I have been in the sport for so many years and have ridden so many different horses for so many people. Let's just say too many to count, especially as I'm not good at maths!

How do you look after all your horses at once?

My horses are extremely well looked after. I have a brilliant back-up team of four people who help me care for them to the very highest standards. I am very hands-on and am very much involved in all the stable chores and the management side. That is all part of it to me. Horsemanship is not just about the riding.

About Pippa

I'm getting a new pony and I don't know what to call it. How do you decide on your horses' names?

I love thinking up new names for our young horses! Sometimes I look back to the names of the parents and link the two together in some way, but sometimes names just come to me.

When I got Redesigned as a youngster, he was the first chestnut I had had for a while, so I nicknamed him Red. When it came to finding a smart competition name I knew I wanted to keep "red" in it, and as he had been bred to be a showjumper, but changed to become an eventer, I thought Redesigned was very suitable.

Ask Pippa

You used to be in the Pony Club. Would you recommend it for young riders?

I would most definitely recommend the Pony Club for any young enthusiast. You learn so much, and you also have such fun and make so many friends. I would highly recommend it.

What is your favourite event? Showjumping, dressage, or cross-county – and why?

I enjoy all three phases, but probably the reason I event is because I love the cross-country. There is no better feeling than having had a great ride around a cross-country course.

Ask Pippa

What's been your most challenging competition to date?

I have had many challenging competitions in my career, but the one that stands out is probably Burghley in 2003, the final leg of the Rolex Grand Slam. From a nerves and personal pressure point of view, I had the high expectations of so many riding on my shoulders, and obviously the hope of scooping up the financial reward if I won. I have never since, and probably never will, have the chance to ride for that sort of amount again. To win the Rolex with two amazing, very special horses, who I am convinced knew what the job entailed, was very definitely my greatest achievement.

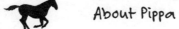

How do you control your nerves before a competition?

I have learned to accept now that nerves are all part of the game, but I used to really struggle with them. Like everyone else, I hate the feeling of nerves and often wonder why I keep putting myself through it. The most comforting thing to remember is most of us suffer from nerves, and to realise they can work for us by being positive energy and adrenalin. They only become negative when we allow ourselves to dwell and think too much about things that might happen.

I try my hardest not to allow my imagination to play tricks on me, like exaggerating the size of a ditch or fences. Before a major competition I will get into a good book, or do su doku puzzle, or chat with friends – anything to avoid thinking negatively.

And I always come back to this saying: 'Think positively about the things you can control, rather than wasting time worrying about the things you can't.'

When you compete, who is your biggest enemy?

I don't have any great rivals when I compete, and I certainly don't like the word enemies. To me it's about trying to do the best job with my horses, getting all three phases right when it really matters. I don't want to have to rely on other people's misfortunes in order to win.

There is no greater feeling than being able to lead from the front and holding onto that lead throughout the competition.

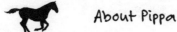 About Pippa

What was your very first event? And how old were you and the horse?

I did plenty of events when I was in the Pony Club, but my first affiliated event was at Tweseldown, where I did a Junior Novice event when I was fifteen, riding my first horse, Sir Barnaby.

In those days ponies were not allowed to affiliate events, if you wanted to event you did it with the Pony Club.

What was the best thing about the Olympics?

I have been very privileged to have been to two Olympics.

They are the pinnacle of any sport and I have many very special memories from both Sydney 2000 and Athens 2004, but probably the best moments were the award ceremonies. Standing on the podium with my fellow team mates, accepting our Olympic medals, really is the icing on the cake. There's an overwhelming feeling of pride and relief, and it makes all the hard work over many years, the good days and disappointing days, all worthwhile.

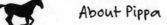

I saw you ride at Badminton last year – what are your plans for the future?

What are my plans? Who knows!!

I seem to be riding as many horses as ever. I am still hungry to do well. One of my main goals is to try and get on the team for the Olympics in London, but I know only too well the ups and downs of horses, how easily they can bang themselves when rolling in the stable just at the wrong time. They're not machines and you can't always fix them quickly.

Long term I am involved with helping run and produce The Billy Stud horses. My husband William and close friend Donal Barnwell set up The Billy Stud over ten years ago. We are not only breeding, but also hopefully producing lots of top competition horses for the future.

Ask Pippa

And as an author, I hope you enjoy and feel you have learned some things from my books, and that you tell all your friends how brilliant they are and tell everyone to buy them so that I can become as famous as JK Rowling. I think one of my plans should be to stop dreaming!!

I love reading your *Tilly's Pony Tails* books. How many more will you write? Do you have a favourite?

I love telling Tilly's story, so let's wait and see. I have eighteen books planned so far, and maybe more to come. I have enjoyed working on all of them, and I have become fond of all the various horses and ponies in the books, but I suppose I am like Tilly in that the special horse to me is Magic Spirit, rather like my Sir Barnaby, he was the first.

Is the character of Tilly based on you?

She was never supposed to be based on me,
although secretly I was that pony-mad little girl
who had all of those dreams and lived and
breathed horses. But I have to say my life with
horses has been better than those dreams – I just
didn't quite figure out how much work was
involved! I hope many of you will be like Tilly and
myself, and share the pleasure in working with,
and being in the company of, these amazing
animals.

Acknowledgements

When Fiona Kennedy at Orion asked me if I would be interested in doing a book answering horse questions which people would send in, I thought 'no problem'. I have a habit of jumping into these projects without quite appreciating the time involved. If my only job was in editorial that wouldn't cause too much of a problem, but as you can all imagine on top of my eventing career, my Billy Stud commitments and, of course, not forgetting Tilly and her pony tales, I have found the 'no problem' answer a massive understatement.

Thanks go to a very understanding team at Orion who know me well enough by now to know that deadlines don't seem to exist in the Funnell household, (I was three months over their deadline with this book!), in particular to Jenny Glencross, editor at Orion Children's Books, who in conjunction with Jenny Kleboe, (William and my secretary for many years, who now seems to have to completely organise our lives) had to do the cracking of the whip and chase me to get finished. Without them there would be no finished article.

I have to confess Lisa Ford, a very good friend, did some of the research for a few of the questions, and thanks must go to her for her assistance.

A huge thanks to all of you who sent in the questions for me to answer – including Jessica, Carrie, Pippa, Emily, Lucy B, Rebecca, Emma, Martha, Megan, Tija K, Kasinia, Lulu, Holly, Vicky, Holly H, Eliza, Beth, Tasha, Sophie, Polly and Lydia, Ella, Olivia, Abigail, Tara, Christina B, Rosie, Jack, Issy, Louisa and Grace B, Shannon, Tash H, Anastasia, Sophie O, Amber, Saffron, Abi, Harriet, Lily, Lucy B, Alys, and many more.

Lastly, but most importantly, I must not forget the thanks I owe to my wonderful horses, who have taught me so much over the years and given me so much pleasure.

Pippa Funnell
Forest Green,
June 2011

Look out for

**Pippa Funnell:
Follow Your Dreams**

Pippa Funnell as you've never seen her before.

Get to know Pippa – her loves, her hates, her friends,
her family. Meet her beautiful horses, and take a sneaky peek
at life on her gorgeous farm. Find out how she prepares
for important competitions, trains and cares for her horses,
and still has the time to write *Tilly's Pony Tails*.

And discover how, with hard work, passion and
determination, you too can follow your dreams,
just like Pippa.

978 1 4440 0266 9

£6.99